THIS BOOK BELONGS TO...

Name:	Age:

Favourite player:

2020/2021

My Predictions...	Actual...

Black Cats' final position:

Black Cats' top scorer:

League One winners:

League One top scorer:

FA Cup winners:

EFL Cup winners:

Contributors: Rob Mason and Peter Rogers

A TWOCAN PUBLICATION

©2020. Published by twocan under licence from Sunderland AFC.

Every effort has been made to ensure the accuracy of information within this publication but the publishers cannot be held responsible for any errors or omissions. Views expressed are those of the authors and do not necessarily represent those of the publishers or the football club. All rights reserved.

ISBN 978-1-913362-81-2

PICTURE CREDITS: Ian Horrocks, Action Images and Press Association.

£9

CONTENTS

LEE 01 BURGE

POSITION: Goalkeeper **DOB:** 9 January 1993
COUNTRY: England

A former Coventry goalkeeper, Lee joined Sunderland in the summer of 2019 and played in three Carabao Cup away victories – including at Premier League clubs Burnley and Sheffield United - before a home debut in the EFL Trophy.

In all, Lee made eleven appearances in his first season at Sunderland, conceding 13 goals. Burge also gained experience on loan to Nuneaton while with Coventry.

CONOR 02 McLAUGHLIN

POSITION: Defender **DOB:** 26 July 1991
COUNTRY: Northern Ireland

A Northern Ireland international, Conor is a right-back who can also operate on the left.

He started his career with Linfield and played for Preston North End, Fleetwood Town and Millwall, as well as having a loan with Shrewsbury Town, before signing for Sunderland in 2019. He made 20 appearances including 12 league starts in his first season on Wearside.

TOM 03 FLANAGAN

POSITION: Defender   **DOB:** 21 October 1991
COUNTRY: Northern Ireland

London born but a Northern Ireland international, Tom can play at full-back or in central defence. He signed a new contract at Sunderland in the summer of 2020 after two years at the club.

Tom began with MK Dons and joined Sunderland from Burton Albion. He has also had loans with Kettering Town, Gillingham, Barnet, Stevenage and Plymouth Argyle.

DENVER
HUME

SOCCER SKILLS

Great goalkeepers are an essential ingredient for successful teams in today's game. They have to excel in all areas of the art of 'keeping and Lee Burge is a great keeper that lives up to these expectations.

DISTRIBUTION
THE BASICS OF GOOD THROWING TECHNIQUE

OVERARM THROW

This is best for covering long distances. The body should be in line with the direction of the throw with the weight on the back foot. The ball should be brought forward in a bowling action with the arm straight.

JAVELIN THROW

This throw is made quickly with a low trajectory. The arm is bent for this throw, the ball is held beside the head and the body is in line with the direction of the throw. The arm is brought forward in a pushing movement with the ball being released at the top.

UNDERARM THROW

The ball is released from a crouching position, with a smooth underarm swing.

Throws do not usually travel as far as kicks but the greater speed and accuracy of throwing can make up for the lack of distance and will help the team retain possession. A player receiving a throw must be able to control it early.

Work hard at distribution and the benefits of this will be seen whenever you are in possession during a match.

EXERCISE ONE

Grab a friend and throw the ball to each other using the various throwing techniques at various distances apart.

EXERCISE TWO

The goalkeeper with the ball uses the various throws to knock another ball off a marker.

EXERCISE THREE

The goalkeepers try to throw the ball through the markers using various throwing techniques.

BOYS OF 1999

The team of 1998-99 didn't just win promotion, they did so with a record 105 points, more than any club had ever managed at that time. New goalkeeper Thomas Sorensen kept a record 29 clean sheets with second choice Andy Marriott also keeping one in his only game. Not only were Sunderland great defensively, conceding only 28 goals in 46 games, in attack they were devastating.

The first choice front two of Niall Quinn and Kevin Phillips were brilliant and even when they missed games through injury their replacements Danny Dichio and Michael Bridges kept the goals coming.

SUPERKEV
STAR PERFORMER

Kevin Phillips was a fantastic goalscorer. Last season, in 2019-20, Jamie Vardy was the Premier League's top scorer with 23 goals. In 1999-2000 Superkev scored 30 Premier League goals, making him Europe's top scorer. That was the season after this 105 point promotion season. In the season before it Phillips had set Sunderland's post-war scoring record with 35 goals.

As promotion was won Superkev missed almost four months of the season through injury but still incredibly managed to score 23 times in 26 league games. Four of those goals came on the night promotion was won with a 5-2 victory at Bury.

Both Dichio and Bridges scored twice each in a stunning 7-0 victory over Oxford United. Midfielder Alex Rae also got two goals that day with Mickey Gray also scoring. Gray played for England during the season as did Super Kevin Phillips.

With Peter Reid as manager Sunderland also reached the semi-final of the League Cup, which was then known as the Worthington Cup. In the semi-final Sunderland narrowly lost out to Leicester City who were managed by future Sunderland boss Martin O'Neill.

In the league, Sunderland finished 18 points ahead of runners-up Bradford City. When Sunderland went to Bradford, goalkeeper Sorensen had to go off injured. Sunderland did not have a goalkeeper on the bench so centre-forward Niall Quinn went in goal and helped keep a clean sheet - having already scored the winner. Quinn was Player of the Year which was no surprise, as in a brilliant team, everything revolved around him.

BAILEY 05 WRIGHT

POSITION: Defender   **DOB:** 28 July 1992
COUNTRY: Australia

Capped 24 times by Australia to the start of this season, Bailey played against England at the Stadium of Light in 2016 and was part of his country's squad at the 2014 FIFA World Cup in Brazil.

The composed and commanding central defender signed for Sunderland in the summer of 2020 after making a positive impression on loan from Bristol City last season.

04 JORDAN WILLIS

POSITION: Defender   **DOB:** 24 August 1994
COUNTRY: England

A speedy and decisive defender who joined in 2019 from his home city club Coventry.

Jordan is a former England Under 18 and 19 international and was only 17 years and 72 days old when he debuted for the Sky Blues in 2011. Now an experienced player, he is a key man in Sunderland's defence as well as being a threat at attacking set-pieces.

SQUAD 2020-21

MAX 06 POWER

POSITION: Midfielder **DOB:** 27 July 1993
COUNTRY: England

A driving force in midfield, the former Tranmere Rovers and Wigan Athletic player has shown himself to be a determined captain.

Capable of scoring with spectacular long-range shots, Max scored in a penalty shoot-out on his debut for Tranmere in 2011. Twice a League One winner with Wigan, he will aim for a third promotion with Sunderland this season.

CHRIS 07 MAGUIRE

POSITION: Midfielder **DOB:** 16 January 1989
COUNTRY: Scotland

Top scorer and top assist-maker last season, Maguire is the magician in the team. He can conjure up spectacular goals and open up defences.

A full international with Scotland, he won promotion from League Two with Oxford in 2016. He has also played for Aberdeen, Derby County, Sheffield Wednesday, Rotherham United and Bury as well as having loans with Kilmarnock, Portsmouth and Coventry City.

GOAL
OF THE SEASON

MAX POWER

SHEFFIELD UTD 0-1 SUNDERLAND
CARABAO CUP THIRD ROUND

POWER'S PILE-DRIVER

Sunderland scored some cracking goals last season but surely none better than Max Power's goal at Sheffield United that helped Sunderland reach the fourth round of the Carabao Cup.

Power's ninth-minute goal proved to be the only one of the tie as Sunderland played well to keep a clean sheet and win away to a Premier League side for the second round in a row, having already won at Burnley.

The winning goal at the Blades' Bramall Lane came from a corner. With the penalty area packed, Chris Maguire played the ball to Luke O'Nien just outside the box. O'Nien did well to control the ball and play it to Power who took a touch to steady himself and side-step a defender before giving the keeper absolutely no chance with a blistering shot that flew into the top corner of the net.

Later O'Nien went close to adding a second goal when he hit the post with a left foot shot after Denver Hume did really well to get to the goal-line and pull back a driven low cross for O'Nien to latch onto.

Sunderland goalkeeper Lee Burge had a good game, making some telling saves but Sunderland were full value for their victory and Power's pile-driver was worthy of winning any match.

Three days later Power did it again with a shot from outside the box - this time after being teed up by Charlie Wyke - in a home win over MK Dons.

LYNDEN GOOCH
DONCASTER ROVERS 1-2 SUNDERLAND
LEAGUE ONE

Lynden Gooch's goal was perhaps the most important of the season. Without a win in nine games, Sunderland lacked confidence but after the USA international cut inside, beat a defender with a step-over and curled the ball into the top corner from the edge of the box, Sunderland went on to win the game and go on the best run of the season.

CHRIS MAGUIRE
SUNDERLAND 1-0 IPSWICH TOWN
LEAGUE ONE

Sunderland needed to beat the Tractor Boys to leap-frog them in the table and re-enter the top six on a weekend when international supporters from around the world attended the Stadium of Light. The late winner came from Chris Maguire who smashed home into the bottom corner after Charlie Wyke and Kyle Lafferty combined to set him up.

15

ADULTS

By what mechanism was the League One table decided last season following the Covid-19 pandemic?

1 ANSWER

How many teams in League One for 2020-21 have previously competed in the Premier League?

2 ANSWER

With which club was Ipswich Town manager Paul Lambert once a Champions League winner?

3 ANSWER

Who were the title sponsors of League One before Sky Bet?

4 ANSWER

Prior to moving to the Keepmoat Stadium, where did Doncaster Rovers play their home matches?

5 ANSWER

Can you name the former Premier League striker who is now owner and chairman of a League One club?

6 ANSWER

Of all the 2020-21 League One clubs, who was the most recent winner of the FA Cup?

7 ANSWER

When Luton Town won the League One title in 2018-19 how many points did they amass - 92, 93 or 94?

8 ANSWER

At which League One ground will you find 'The Milton End'?

9 ANSWER

Can you name the striker who left a League One club in the summer of 2020 after scoring over a century of goals for them?

10 ANSWER

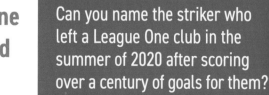

V KIDS

ANSWERS ON PAGE 62

Challenge your favourite grown-up and find out which of you is the biggest League One brain!
The adults' questions are on the left page and the kids' questions are on the right page.

1 Which League One club play their home games at Home Park?

ANSWER

2 Who won promotion to League One for 2020-21 via last season's League Two Play-Offs?

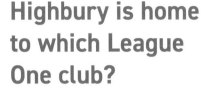

3 Which two clubs won automatic promotion from League One last season?

ANSWER

4 Highbury is home to which League One club?

5 Who is the manager of Portsmouth?

6 How many Welsh clubs are competing in League One in 2020-21?

ANSWER

7 Steve Evans is the manager of which League One team?

8 Which League One stadium has the largest capacity?

9 How many League One clubs have the word 'City' in their name?

ANSWER

10 MK Dons' manager Russell Martin played international football for which country?

Fill the page with your footy goals and dreams, no matter how big or small, and then start working on how to accomplish them!

We've started you off...

1. Visit the Stadium of Light

2. Complete 50 keepy-uppies

FOOTY BUCKET LIST

GRANT LEADBITTER

ANSWERS ON PAGE 6

WHO ARE YER?

Can you figure out the identity of all these SAFC stars?

GEORGE 08 DOBSON

POSITION: Midfielder **DOB:** 15 November 1992
COUNTRY: England

A hard-working and mobile midfielder, Dobson was an academy player with Arsenal and West Ham United before moving to Walsall on loan.

After a brief spell with Sparta Rotterdam he signed for Walsall in January 2018 and was later sold to Sunderland in the summer of 2019. A former captain of his age group at Arsenal, George captained Walsall when he was just 20.

09 CHARLIE WYKE

POSITION: Striker **DOB:** 6 December 1992
COUNTRY: England

A Middlesbrough-born centre-forward, Charlie joined Sunderland in 2018 from Bradford City. He had 73 league goals to his name at the start of this season, nine for Sunderland with all but ten of the others for Carlisle United and Bradford City.

Charlie became Sunderland's first-ever fourth substitute in a game when he came on during extra-time in the 2018 Checkatrade trophy final at Wembley.

LYNDEN 11 GOOCH

POSITION: Forward **DOB:** 24 December 1995
COUNTRY: USA

A USA international who has been associated with Sunderland since he was ten, Lynden always plays with great commitment and has the quality to provide telling moments in games.

Often used in wide midfield positions, he can also operate centrally as well as being able to play as a striker. In his younger years Lynden played for Gateshead and Doncaster Rovers on loan.

AIDEN 10 O'BRIEN

POSITION: Forward **DOB:** 4 October 1993
COUNTRY: Republic of Ireland

Born in Islington, London, Aiden is from an Irish family and qualifies for the Republic of Ireland through his grandparents.

At Under 17 level he had the chance to represent England but preferred to play for Ireland who he went on to score for on his full debut against Poland in 2018. He joined Sunderland last summer after over 200 games for Millwall.

PREPARING FOR ACTION

Football matches may well be scheduled for 90 minutes but there are many days of preparation that go into making sure that Phil Parkinson's men are at their physical and mental peak when they cross the white line to represent Sunderland AFC.

Like all Football League clubs, the Black Cats' pre-match planning it meticulous. The manager of course has final say as to who makes his starting line-up but the boss is ably assisted by a backroom staff of coaches, sports scientists, strength and conditioning experts, physiotherapists and nutritionists who all play their part in helping fine tune the players ahead of the manager's team selection.

The majority of the squads' preparations take place at the club's training ground and that all begins when the players report back for pre-season training.

Although the modern-day player has little down-time in terms of maintaining his overall fitness, pre-season really is a vital time for footballers to build themselves up to remain as fit, strong and healthy as possible for the challenging season that awaits.

The pre-season schedule often begins with a series of fitness tests. The results of those tests enables the club's coaching and fitness staff to assess each player's condition and level of fitness to ensure they are given the right work load during the pre-season programme.

When it comes to winning football matches, it is well known that both hard work and practice are two essential ingredients to success. However, in terms of strength and fitness, then rest, recovery and diet also have crucial parts to play in a footballer's wellbeing.

The modern game now sees technology playing its part in training too - prior to beginning their training sessions, the players are provided with a GPS tracking system and heart rate analysis monitors ensuring that all that they do in a training session can be measured, monitored and reviewed.

On-pitch training drills and gym work is now enhanced further with players often taking part in yoga and pilates classes while always receiving expert advice in terms of their diet, rest and mental welfare.

CHRIS
MAGUIRE

SOCCER SKILLS
DEFENDING

Defending is an art - not as spectacular as swerving a free kick around the wall into the net or floating a crossfield pass into the path of an oncoming wingback - but nevertheless, just as important. Every successful team has a solid defence and can defend as a team.

Defenders must also master the art of defending one on one...

EXERCISE ONE

Two adjacent 10m x 10m grids have two players, X and Y at the opposite ends of the grids. X plays the ball to Y, who is then allowed to attack defender X with the ball. Y's target is to be able to stop the ball, under control, on the opposite end line. Defender X has to try to stop this happening. Y is encouraged to be direct and run at X with the ball.

KEY FACTORS

1. Do not approach the attacker square on. Adopt a sideways stance which enables rapid forward and backwards movement.

2. Do not dive in. Be patient and wait for your opponent to make a mistake. Always be on your toes.

3. Threaten the ball without actually committing to a tackle. Pretending to tackle can often panic the opponent!

4. Tackle when you are sure you will win it!

EXERCISE TWO

Here the game is progressed to a two v two situation when X1 and X2 play as a team against Y1 and Y2.

The same target is used for this game - the players have to stand on the opposite line with the ball, either by dribbling past their opponents or by passing the ball through them.

The same key factors are relevant here with the addition of two more:

5. Covering your defending partner when he is being attacked.

6. Communication between the two defenders is vital.

If a team can get these points of defending right, throughout the side, they will become very difficult to beat.

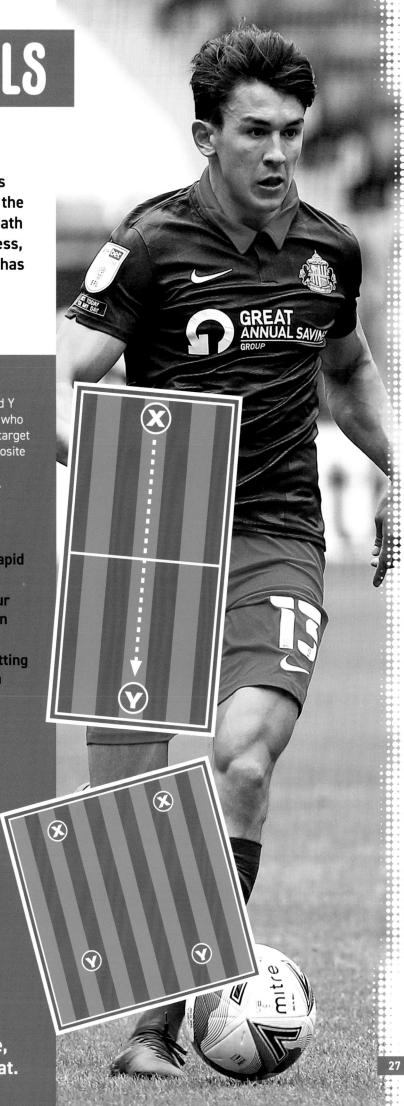

Take our quick-fire personality test to see where Phil Parkinson would utilise your skills in the SAFC line-up...

WHICH FOOTBALLER ARE YOU?

1. What is your favourite activity at the park?

a. Leaping around
b. Practicing my heading
c. Lots of non-stop running
d. Scoring goals

2. What is your biggest strength?

a. My height
b. My strength
c. My stamina
d. My speed

3. Which would you rather win?

a. A game of catch
b. A weight lifting contest
c. A long distance run
d. A sprint race

4. You score a goal! How do you celebrate?

a. I turn and punch the air
b. I clench my fist in delight
c. I high-five a teammate
d. I slide on my knees

5. How would the opposition describe you?

a. Hard to beat
b. Determined to succeed
c. All-action
d. Lethal in front of goal

6. What's your favourite move?

a. Springing high to catch under pressure
b. A sliding tackle
c. Playing the perfect through ball
d. Spinning away from my marker

7. What is the key to winning a game?

a. Keeping a clean sheet

b. Winning your individual battles

c. Maintaining possession

d. Taking chances that come your way

MOSTLY As

You would clearly be a safe pair of hands in goal. Watch out Lee Burge, there's competition here for the No1 shirt!

8. What is your favourite number?

a. One

b. Five

c. Seven

d. Nine

MOSTLY Bs

Sounds like you are a young Jordan Willis in the making - there could well be a role for you in the SAFC back three...

MOSTLY Cs

You could comfortably take your place in the heart of midfield and help make things tick. Move over Max Power!

9. How would you describe your style of play?

a. Disciplined

b. Fully committed

c. Relentless

d. Technically gifted

10. What do your teammates call you?

a. Secure

b. Reliable

c. Energetic

d. Mr/Miss goals

MOSTLY Ds

Looks like we have a budding Aiden O'Brien on our hands! Who do you fancy partnering in attack?

LUKE 13 O'NIEN

POSITION: Midfielder / full-back   **DOB:** 21 November 1994
COUNTRY: England

Ever popular with the fans due to his whole-hearted effort, impressive ability and evident enjoyment of playing for Sunderland, O'Nien is still rocking all over League One.

Luke came through the youth system at Watford, playing for them in just one league game as a very late substitute in 2014. He also had a loan with Wealdstone before appearing over 100 times for Wycombe Wanderers.

14 JOSH SCOWEN

POSITION: Midfielder   **DOB:** 28 March 1993
COUNTRY: England

Josh made at least 100 appearances for Wycombe Wanderers, Barnsley and QPR who he left to join Sunderland in January 2020.

He played 18 Championship games in the first half of last season before joining Sunderland in January but only started one game before the season was suddenly called off. Josh could well be an influential midfielder this season.

MORGAN 15 FEENEY

POSITION: Defender **DOB:** 8 February 1999
COUNTRY: England

Capped by England at Under 17, 18 and 19 level, Morgan joined Sunderland in the summer after leaving his first club Everton.

A commanding central defender, Morgan played in the Europa League against Italian club Atalanta in 2017 and went on loan to Tranmere at the start of 2020 to gain experience only for injury to restrict him to just one game.

ELLIOT 17 EMBLETON

POSITION: Midfielder **DOB:** 9 April 1999
COUNTRY: England

Elliot started last season well, playing in the opening day draw with Oxford and then in league away wins at Rochdale and Accrington and Carabao Cup victories at Premier League Burnley and Sheffield United before his season came to an end due to injury.

A talented local lad, he has been capped by England up to Under 20 level and gained experience on loan to Grimsby.

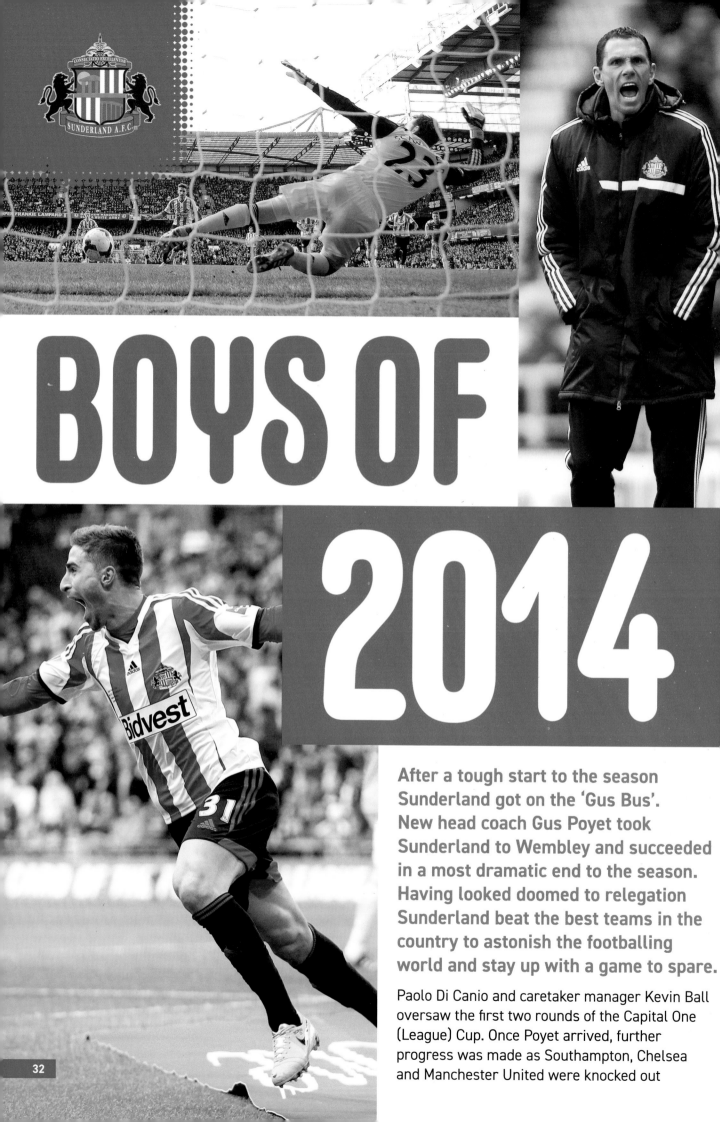

BOYS OF 2014

After a tough start to the season Sunderland got on the 'Gus Bus'. New head coach Gus Poyet took Sunderland to Wembley and succeeded in a most dramatic end to the season. Having looked doomed to relegation Sunderland beat the best teams in the country to astonish the footballing world and stay up with a game to spare.

Paolo Di Canio and caretaker manager Kevin Ball oversaw the first two rounds of the Capital One (League) Cup. Once Poyet arrived, further progress was made as Southampton, Chelsea and Manchester United were knocked out

CONNOR WICKHAM

STAR PERFORMER

Connor Wickham was a sensation when he burst onto the scene as a 16-year-old with Ipswich Town. Signed for a big fee by Steve Bruce he had rarely found the back of the net and been loaned out, but in 2013-14 he paid back his transfer fee with a burst of goals that made him the Premier League Player of the Month.

Five goals in three games, including two at Manchester City and one at Chelsea were followed up by a key assist for Seb Larsson's winner at Manchester United as the England Under 21 international delivered the goods.

- the latter after a dramatic penalty shoot-out at Old Trafford where goalkeeper Vito Mannone was the hero. In the final at Wembley, Sunderland led at half-time thanks to a Fabio Borini goal before two 'worldies' in two minutes from Yaya Toure and Samir Nasri put City ahead with Jesus Navas ending the game as a contest in the 90th minute. Sunderland though had 'Dared to Dream' and the Red and White army had taken over the capital.

The following month, games against Manchester City and a return to the capital to face Chelsea inspired a miracle comeback that even Poyet seemed to feel was impossible. Only a lucky late goal from Nasri stopped Sunderland claiming a shock win at Manchester City.

Three days later Sunderland inflicted title-chasing Chelsea's first-ever home defeat in 78 games under Jose Mourinho by winning 2-1. After thrashing Cardiff 4-0 at home, Sunderland won at Manchester United and secured safety with victory over West Brom. It had been the greatest of great escapes.

COLOUR

AIDEN

O'BRIEN

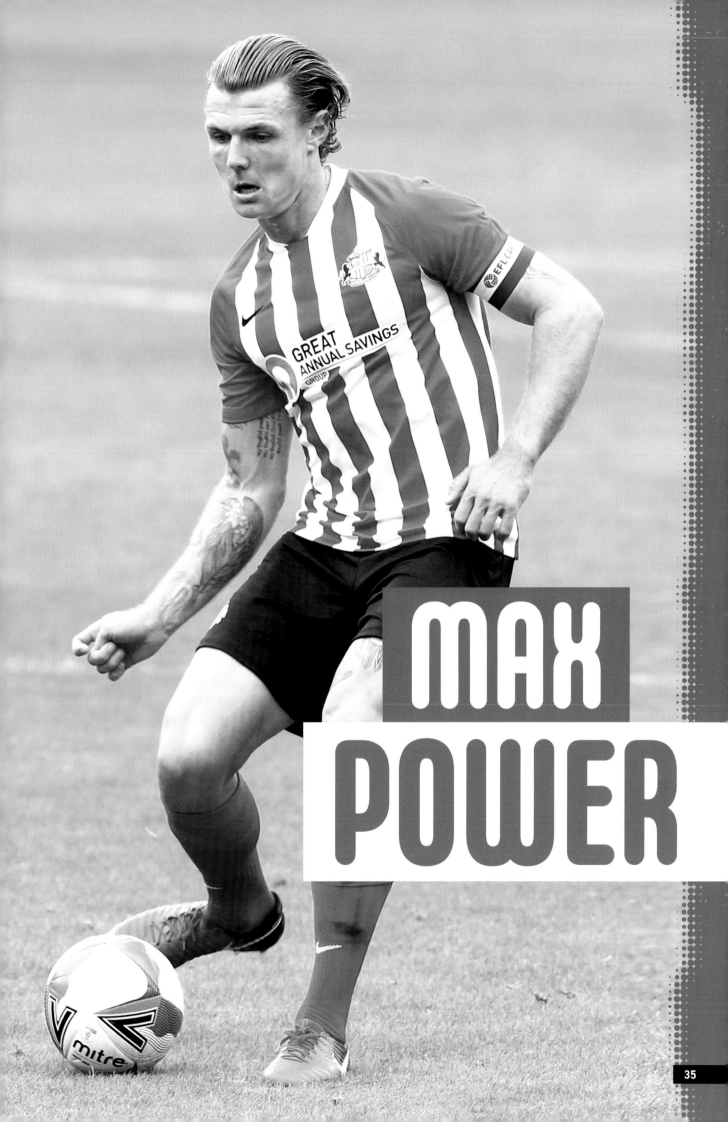

MAX
POWER

HEY REF!

Do you always know what the officials are signalling?

Take a look at these and see if you are up to the job...

ANSWERS ON PAGE 62

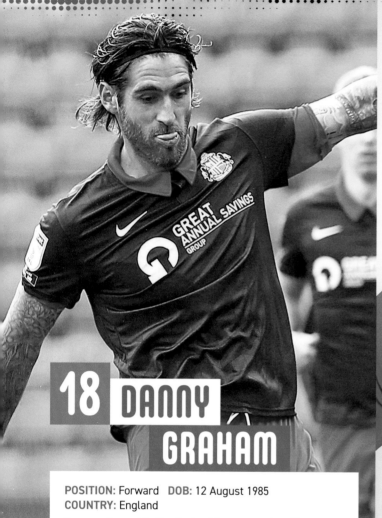

18 DANNY GRAHAM

POSITION: Forward **DOB:** 12 August 1985
COUNTRY: England

Danny returned to Sunderland for a second spell on 7 September. Gateshead born, Danny was previously at Sunderland in the Premier League from 2013 to 2016.

Since then he was with Blackburn Rovers, who he had first joined on loan from Sunderland. Graham grabbed 57 goals in 191 games for Rovers, 14 of them as they won promotion from League One in 2018.

ARBENIT 19 XHEMAJLI

POSITION: Defender **DOB:** 23 April 1998
COUNTRY: Kosovo

Centre-back Arbenit signed from Swiss side Neuchatel Xamax for whom he made his debut in an amazing 21-0 away win over Union-Sportive Montfaucon in the Swiss Cup in August 2017.

Arbenit went on to play over 50 games for Xamax scoring a couple of goals including a late winner at FC Sion. He made his full international debut for Kosovo in 2019.

REMI 20 MATTHEWS

POSITION: Goalkeeper   **DOB:** 10 February 1994
COUNTRY: England

Remi arrived in the summer of 2020, signed by Phil Parkinson who he had played for at Bolton.

Born in Norfolk, he started with his local club Norwich City. Although he did not get a game for the Canaries, Remi gained the experience of 69 games on loan for four clubs before joining Bolton who he had initially been on loan with.

JACK 21 DIAMOND

POSITION: Midfielder   **DOB:** 12 January 2000
COUNTRY: England

A highly promising winger, Jack excelled on loan last season to Harrogate Town.

He helped the Yorkshire side to gain a place in the EFL with a goal and Man of the Match award in the National League Play-Off final at Wembley against Notts County, a team he had played against for Sunderland in the Checkatrade Trophy in 2018.

There are five Samson the Cats hiding in the crowd as Sunderland fans celebrate winning the FA Cup at Wembley in 1973. Can you find him?

CLASSIC FANTASTIC

JOSH
SCOWEN

Can you find the eight differences between these two photos?

SPOT THE DIFFERENCE

Here are our predictions for the 2020-21 season, see if you agree!

2020-21

PREMIER LEAGUE

OUR PREDICTION FOR PREMIER LEAGUE WINNERS:

LEICESTER CITY

YOUR PREDICTION:

OUR PREDICTION FOR PREMIER LEAGUE RUNNERS-UP:

LIVERPOOL

YOUR PREDICTION:

CHAMPIONSHIP

OUR PREDICTION FOR CHAMPIONSHIP WINNERS:

WATFORD

YOUR PREDICTION:

OUR PREDICTION FOR CHAMPIONSHIP RUNNERS-UP:

SWANSEA CITY

YOUR PREDICTION:

LEAGUE ONE

OUR PREDICTION FOR LEAGUE ONE WINNERS:
SUNDERLAND

YOUR PREDICTION:

OUR PREDICTION FOR LEAGUE ONE RUNNERS-UP:
IPSWICH TOWN

YOUR PREDICTION:

FA CUP & EFL CUP

OUR PREDICTION FOR FA CUP WINNERS:
ARSENAL

YOUR PREDICTION:

OUR PREDICTION FOR EFL CUP WINNERS:
BRIGHTON & HA

YOUR PREDICTION:

PREDICTIONS

23 GRANT LEADBITTER

POSITION: Midfielder **DOB:** 7 January 1986
COUNTRY: England

A talented footballer who played for England at five levels up to Under 21 level, Grant was a product of the Sunderland youth system and played 123 times for Sunderland before leaving in 2009.

After 126 games for Ipswich and 244 for Middlesbrough, he returned to Sunderland in January 2019. Grant has won promotion from the Championship on both Wearside and Teesside.

WILL 22 GRIGG

POSITION: Striker **DOB:** 3 July 1991
COUNTRY: Northern Ireland

Northern Ireland international Grigg was born in Solihull, Birmingham and qualifies for Northern Ireland through his grandfather.

He was League One's top scorer in 2015-16 for Wigan and at the end of that season, a song called 'Will Grigg's on Fire' reached number seven in the itunes chart! At the start of this season he had 109 league goals, including five for Sunderland.

DAN 24 NEILL

POSITION: Midfielder   DOB: 13 December 2001
COUNTRY: England

A South Shields-born attacking midfielder, Dan always looks to make penetrating runs and passes.

An England international at Under 16 level, Dan got a very brief taste of first team involvement as a sub at Morecambe in the Checkatrade Trophy in November 2018 and after catching the eye in pre-season looked set to push for more first team action in 2020-21.

29 CIERAN DUNNE

POSITION: Midfielder   DOB: 8 February 2000
COUNTRY: Republic of Ireland

Signed from Falkirk in July 2019, Dunne was born in Linlithgow in Scotland but has represented the Republic of Ireland at Under 18 level.

Cieran made six appearances for Falkirk in the Scottish Championship plus two in cup competitions. He also played for Hutchison Vale and Forth Valley Football Academy before coming to Sunderland while still in his teens.

LYNDEN GOOCH

SOCCER SKILLS
CHEST CONTROL

Controlling the ball quickly and with minimum fuss in order to get the ball where you want it, so you can pass or shoot, can be the difference between a good player and a top class player.

EXERCISE ONE

Grab two of your mates to start the exercise. A and C stand 10yds apart and have a ball each, ready to act as servers.

B works first. B must run towards A who serves the ball for B to control with the chest and pass back to A. B then turns, runs to C and repeats the exercise.

Once B has worked for 30 seconds all the players rotate.

KEY FACTORS

1. Look to control the ball as early as possible.
2. Get in line with the ball.
3. Keep eyes on the ball.
4. Relax the body on impact with the ball to cushion it.

EXERCISE TWO

In this exercise there are 5 servers positioned around a 15yd square. At one side of the square there is a goal.

T starts in the middle of the square. S1 serves first, throwing the ball in the air towards T. T must control the ball with the chest and try to shoot past the goalkeeper, as soon as T has shot on goal they must prepare for the next serve from S2.

Once T has received a ball from every server the players rotate positions - the same key factors apply.

Players who can control a ball quickly, putting the ball in a position for a shot or pass, give themselves and their teammates the extra valuable seconds required in today's intense style of play.

In which season did Sunderland last win promotion from the third tier?

11 ANSWER

Ipswich Town were last crowed third tier champions in 1956-57 - true or false?

12 ANSWER

Can you name the two current League One clubs that West Ham captain Mark Noble has played on loan for?

13 ANSWER

Which League One club is famously known for being mentioned in a 1980s advert for the Milk Marketing Board?

14 ANSWER

Which League One club used to play their home matches at the Manor Ground?

15 ANSWER

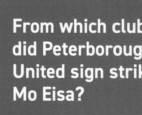

Other than Peterborough United, which two other clubs has Darren Ferguson managed?

16 ANSWER

At which club did Sunderland manager Phil Parkinson begin his managerial career?

17 ANSWER

From which club did Peterborough United sign striker Mo Eisa?

18 ANSWER

When League One rivals Portsmouth and Plymouth Argyle meet, what is the match known as?

19 ANSWER

From which club have MK Dons loaned striker Carlton Morris for the 2020-21 season?

20 ANSWER

V KIDS

Challenge your favourite grown-up and find out which of you is the biggest League One brain!
The adults' questions are on the left page and the kids' questions are on the right page.

ANSWERS ON PAGE 62

Who is the manager of Oxford United?

11

Which club play their home matches at the KCOM Stadium?

12

How many 2020-21 League One clubs are based in London?

13 ANSWER

Which League One club's nickname is 'The Imps'?

14

Can you name the League One club that plays their home fixtures at London Road?

15

Shrewsbury Town manager Sam Ricketts played international football for which country?

16 ANSWER

What is Burton Albion's nickname?

17

Bristol Rovers are famous for playing in what type of shirts?

18

Which club has the largest ground capacity - Hull City or Doncaster Rovers?

19 ANSWER

Who is the manager of Swindon Town?

20

51

BOYS OF 1973

THE EMPIRE STADIUM, WEMBLEY

The Football Association
Challenge Cup
Competition

FINAL TIE

SAT., MAY 5, 1973

TURNSTILES
G
ENTRANCE
66
WEST
STANDING
ENCLOSURE

KICK-OFF 3 p.m.
YOU ARE ADVISED TO TAKE UP
YOUR POSITION BY 2.30 p.m.

J.S.lut. CHAIRMAN
WEMBLEY STADIUM LTD

STANDING
£1.00

SEE PLAN AND CONDITIONS ON

TO BE RETAINED

Sunderland didn't just win the FA Cup in 1973, they did so by knocking out three of the top teams in the country. After beating Notts County and Reading, Manchester City were defeated in a replay eventually voted 'Match of the Century.' Luton Town were then eliminated before Arsenal were defeated in the semi-final. At Wembley the opponents were Leeds United who were a top side of the time. Sunderland were very much the underdogs but won 1-0.

Shortly before Christmas Sunderland had been struggling near the bottom of what we now call the Championship. Once Bob Stokoe took over

DAVE WATSON

STAR PERFORMER

The 1973 FA Cup final is rightly remembered for Ian Porterfield's goal and Jim Montgomery's legendary double save but it was centre-half Dave Watson who was Man of the Match.

Watson had been a centre-forward when he was signed as Sunderland's first-ever £100,000 player, but he had been converted back to his original defensive position during the cup-winning campaign. During the cup final his heading, tackling and covering were all brilliant. Dave went on to win the first 14 of his 65 England caps with Sunderland. He was inducted into the SAFC Hall of Fame in 2020.

as manager there was a dramatic improvement. Sunderland had a lot of exciting young players and Stokoe allowed them to show their flair and brought in a handful of experienced players to add to the team.

Forwards Billy Hughes and Dennis Tueart tore teams apart with their pace and directness. Centre-forward Vic Halom scored the goal of the cup run against Manchester City and opened the scoring in the semi-final.

In goal Jim Montgomery was spectacularly fantastic. Full-backs Dick Malone and Ron Guthrie were defensively solid and liked to get forward. Alongside defensive king-pin Dave Watson Ritchie Pitt was strong and dependable. In midfield, young Micky Horswill was the man who stopped the top stars of the opposition from playing while schemer Ian Porterfield was the great creator who scored the only goal of the final. Captain Bobby Kerr was hard-working, clever on the ball and the man who lifted the FA Cup.

SQUAD 2020-21

JAKE 34 HACKETT

POSITION: Midfielder **DOB:** 10 January 2000
COUNTRY: England

Jake has been with Sunderland since first coming to the Academy as an eight-year old. He played in pre-season having gained experience with two loans to Whitby Town.

In 2018-19 Jake played three games in the Checkatrade Trophy having appeared in the same competition for Sunderland Under 21s the season before.

DENVER 33 HUME

POSITION: Defender **DOB:** 11 August 1998
COUNTRY: England

A successful product of the Sunderland Academy, which the local lad has been with since he was 10, Denver made last season his breakthrough campaign as a regular first-teamer.

Having made his first team debut in the final game of the 2017-18 season, in 2018-19 Hume appeared eleven times before establishing himself as first choice left-back or left wing-back in 2019-20.

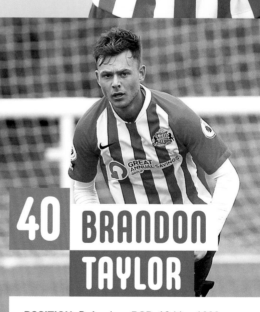

40 BRANDON TAYLOR

POSITION: Defender **DOB:** 10 May 1999
COUNTRY: England

Brandon started the season with a new contract, hoping for another chance after an impressive 120 minutes in an FA Cup tie at Gillingham that went to extra-time.

The Gateshead lad has been with Sunderland since he was eleven. Brandon can play at right-back or centre-back and is well suited to playing on the right of a back three.

ANTHONY 43
PATTERSON

POSITION: Goalkeeper   **DOB:** 10 May 2000
COUNTRY: England

A talented young keeper who played half an hour at the Stadium of Light in a pre-season friendly with Carlisle United. Newcastle born, Anthony has been with the academy since he was nine.

Brave and often capable of spectacular stops, he is likely to be in high demand from clubs wanting to take him on loan as the youngster looks to gain experience.

BENJI
KIMPIOKA

POSITION: Striker   **DOB:** 21 February 2000
COUNTRY: Sweden

Benji re-signed for Sunderland early in October and instantly hit the goals trail with braces in his first two Under 23 games.

A Sweden U21 international, Benji came to Sunderland after starting with IK Sirius from Uppsala, near Stockholm. A speed-merchant capable of the unpredictable, he scored his first league goal with a last-minute equaliser against Coventry last season.

JARGON BUSTER

Here is a list of footy jargon. All but one of the terms are hidden in the grid...

can you work out which is missing?

- All To Play For
- Back Of The Net
- Bags Of Pace
- Big Game Player
- Box-To-Box
- Class Act
- Derby Day
- Dinked In
- Early Doors
- Funny Old Game
- Game Of Two Halves
- Handbags
- Hat-Trick
- Hollywood Pass
- Keep It Tight
- Massive Game
- Midfield General
- Natural Goalscorer
- Row Z
- Worldy

A	S	M	Z	U	C	E	M	A	G	E	V	I	S	S	A	M
V	A	W	T	B	X	O	W	A	C	V	T	S	V	Y	B	N
P	O	I	B	Y	D	I	N	K	E	D	I	N	B	R	Q	A
R	L	Q	C	J	K	X	Z	E	F	M	L	F	J	N	E	T
O	G	F	W	K	C	I	R	T	T	A	H	C	S	A	Z	U
E	X	B	H	D	A	V	A	P	N	H	X	G	B	J	E	R
T	K	A	L	L	T	O	P	L	A	Y	F	O	R	D	C	A
I	R	C	P	M	E	Q	M	O	L	R	X	G	H	O	A	L
F	L	K	D	N	U	R	A	S	T	T	P	K	Q	C	P	G
U	F	O	N	Z	Y	D	I	W	O	M	W	Y	I	B	F	O
N	H	F	W	Z	O	E	S	B	B	U	N	E	H	L	O	A
N	J	T	G	O	B	N	O	D	F	F	X	K	A	D	S	L
Y	Z	H	S	V	R	X	M	A	G	V	O	R	N	I	G	S
O	X	E	A	D	C	L	H	H	G	A	E	U	D	Z	A	C
L	B	N	K	Q	J	L	D	C	J	N	K	A	B	I	B	O
D	D	E	R	B	Y	D	A	Y	E	E	S	P	A	L	B	R
G	W	T	E	U	O	I	P	G	J	I	O	J	G	S	M	E
A	C	I	O	K	I	R	D	Y	U	X	K	T	S	F	A	R
M	H	W	V	Y	B	L	T	B	P	C	H	F	O	R	R	A
E	O	P	C	D	E	E	T	G	E	G	Q	B	L	P	E	N
V	G	C	M	I	H	A	F	M	I	E	K	Y	V	Z	G	L
H	J	B	F	D	W	A	R	T	X	I	D	H	D	C	T	D
L	X	D	M	O	A	S	T	A	S	O	L	G	A	T	C	R
V	I	A	Q	K	Y	I	H	S	O	D	W	J	H	Y	A	Q
M	P	F	E	Z	P	R	G	R	G	U	N	F	M	I	S	G
Z	I	N	Q	E	J	N	S	L	J	P	I	K	Z	Y	S	O
D	B	S	E	V	L	A	H	O	W	T	F	O	E	M	A	G
A	E	K	T	X	S	L	T	E	M	X	K	W	U	L	L	I
S	U	S	N	Q	L	U	W	E	A	B	V	R	S	P	C	O
T	A	Y	O	R	S	F	I	T	W	Y	O	T	A	N	B	M
B	H	O	L	L	Y	W	O	O	D	P	A	S	S	U	T	I

JORDAN WILLIS

Want to leap like Lee Burge, have the strength of Jordan Willis or boast the endurance of Max Power? Build up your strength for action with our...

30 DAY

Day 1
Right let's get started! 10 squats, 25 star jumps, 10 sit-ups - all before school!

Day 2
Make your mum a brew before going out to practice your keepy-uppies

Day 3
10 squats
50 star jumps
10 sit-ups

Day 4
How about swapping the crisps in your lunchbox for an apple?

Day 5
Take a one mile ride on your bike

Day 6
75 star jumps
15 sit-ups
15 press-ups

Day 7
Help clean the car before going out to play headers and volleys with your friends

Day 8
75 star jumps
15 sit-ups
15 press-ups
Before and after school now!

Day 9
Walk to school rather than take the bus

Day 10
Head to the swimming pool for a 30-minute swim

Day 11
100 star jumps
20 sit-ups
20 press-ups
Twice a day now, don't forget!

Day 12
Make sure you trade one of your fizzy drinks for a glass of water today

Day 13
Jog to the shop for your mum... before playing any video games!

Day 14
Give a hand around the house before kicking your ball against the wall 500 times

Day 15
Time to increase those exercises!
25 squats
25 sit-ups
25 press-ups
Before and after school!

Day 16
Take a nice paced two-mile jog today

Day 17
25 squats
150 star jumps
25 press-ups
Remember, before and after school

Day 18
Cycle to school rather than rely on the bus or a lift

Day 19
30 squats
150 star jumps
30 press-ups
Twice a day too!

Day 20
Get out and practice those free-kicks, practice makes perfect remember...

Day 21
Get peddling! Time for a two-mile trip on two wheels today

Day 22
Upping the workload now...
40 squats, 40 sit-ups
40 press-ups
Before and after school!

Day 23
Wave goodbye to the chips - ask for a nice salad for lunch today

Day 24
40 squats
40 sit-ups
40 press-ups
Twice a day, don't forget...

Day 25
Time to get pounding the streets - the jogging is up to three miles today

Day 26
45 star jumps
45 sit-ups
45 press-ups

Day 27
Time to swap those sweets and biscuits for some fruit

Day 28
45 star jumps
45 sit-ups
45 press-ups

Day 29
You're getting fitter and fitter now! Keep up the squats and star jumps plus join an after-school sports club - ideally football!

Day 30
Well done - you made it!
50 squats, 50 sit-ups and 50 press-ups!
These are the core ingredients to your success

CHALLENGE
to improve your all-round footy fitness!

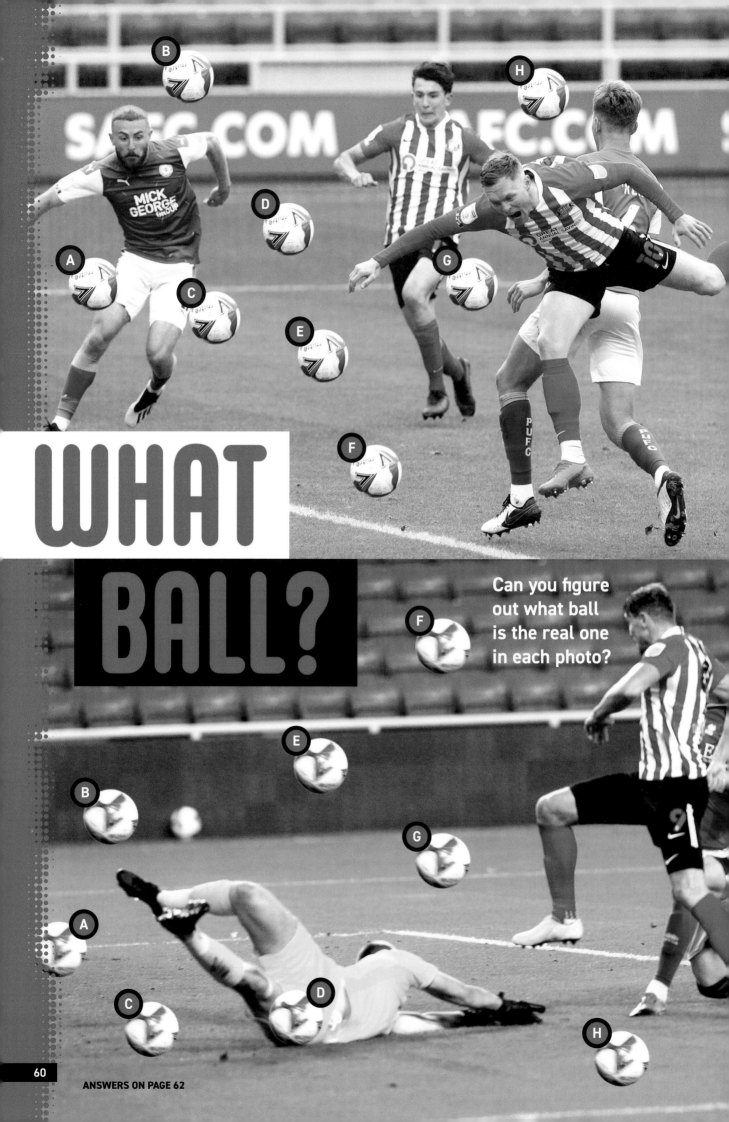

WHAT BALL?

Can you figure out what ball is the real one in each photo?

DANNY GRAHAM

ANSWERS

PAGE 16 · ADULTS V KIDS

Adults

1. Points-per-game. 2. Nine - Blackpool, Charlton Athletic, Hull City, Ipswich Town, Portsmouth, Sunderland, Swindon Town, Wigan Athletic and MK Dons as Wimbledon. 3. Borussia Dortmund. 4. Coca-Cola. 5. Belle Vue. 6. Lee Power - the Swindon chairman formally played for Norwich City in the Premier League. 7. Wigan Athletic in 2013. 8. 94. 9. Fratton Park, Portsmouth. 10. Ian Henderson, Rochdale.

Kids

1. Plymouth Argyle. 2. Northampton Town. 3. Coventry City and Rotherham United. 4. Fleetwood Town. 5. Kenny Jacket. 6. None. 7. Gillingham. 8. Stadium of Light, Sunderland. 9. Two - Hull City and Lincoln City. 10. Scotland.

PAGE 20 · WHO ARE YER?

1. Bailey Wright. 2. Danny Graham.
3. Luke O'Nien. 4. Will Grigg.
5. Josh Scowen. 6. Jordan Willis.
7. Lynden Gooch. 8. Max Power.
9. Denver Hume. 10. Aiden O'Brien.

PAGE 36 · HEY REF

1. Direct free kick. 2. Indirect free kick.
3. Yellow card - Caution. 4. Red card - Sending off.
5. Obstruction. 6. Substitution. 7. Offside/foul.
8. Penalty. 9. Offside location. 10. Play on.

PAGE 40
CLASSIC FANTASTIC →

PAGE 43
SPOT THE DIFFERENCE →

PAGE 50 · ADULTS V KIDS

Adults

11. 1987/88. 12. True. 13. Hull City and Ipswich Town. 14. Accrington Stanley. 15. Oxford United. 16. Preston North End and Doncaster Rovers. 17. Colchester United. 18. Bristol City. 19. The Dockyard Derby. 20. Norwich City.

Kids

11. Karl Robinson. 12. Hull City. 13. Two - AFC Wimbledon and Charlton Athletic. 14. Lincoln City. 15. Peterborough United. 16. Wales. 17. The Brewers. 18. Blue and white quartered shirts. 19. Hull City. 20. Richie Wellen.

PAGE 56 · JARGON BUSTER

Big Game Player.

PAGE 60 · WHAT BALL?

TOP: Ball C.
BOTTOM: Ball A.